4TH OF JULY DOT MARKERS ACTIVITY BOOK

35 4th of July illustrations to color with dot markers

THIS BOOK BELONGS TO

TIPS

1. Position a piece of paper or cardboard under the page to avoid bleed-through

2. You can cut each page along the dotted line on the back and hang them where you want

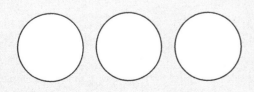

KINDRELL
Land Press

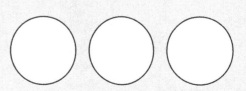

DISCOVER ALL OUR BOOKS

Scan this QR code to find them

KINDRELL Land Press

FOLLOW US ON INSTAGRAM

@ KINDRELLLANDPRESS

to keep up to date with our new releseas,
share your colored artwork with us and get bonuses!

UNCLE
SAM

FIRECRACKERS

BALLOONS

HAMBURGER

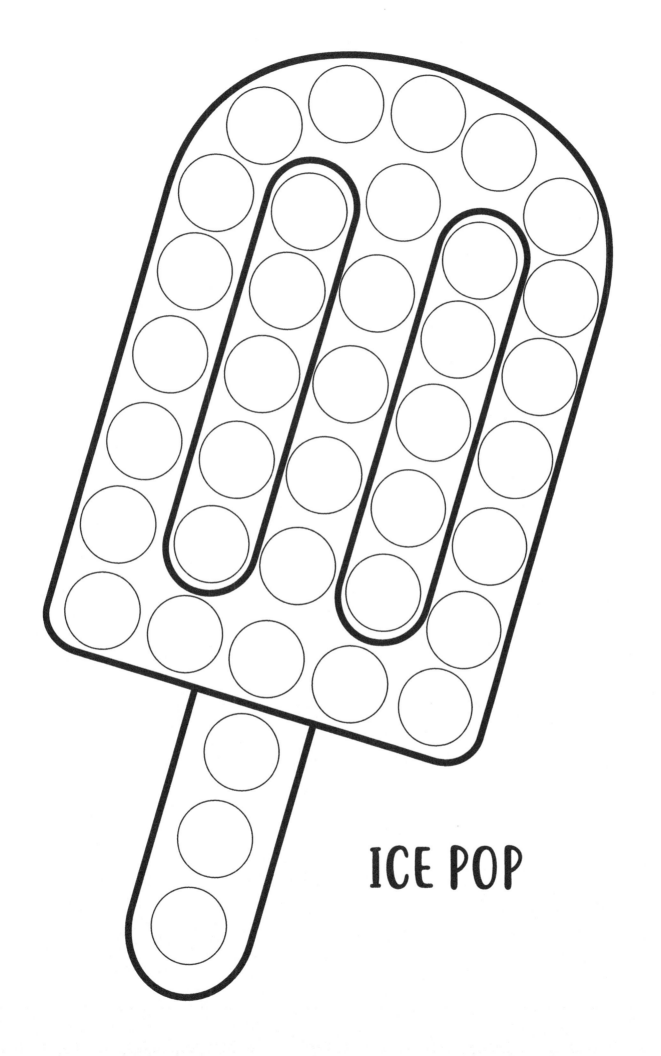

ICE POP

PARTY
HATS

HOT DOG

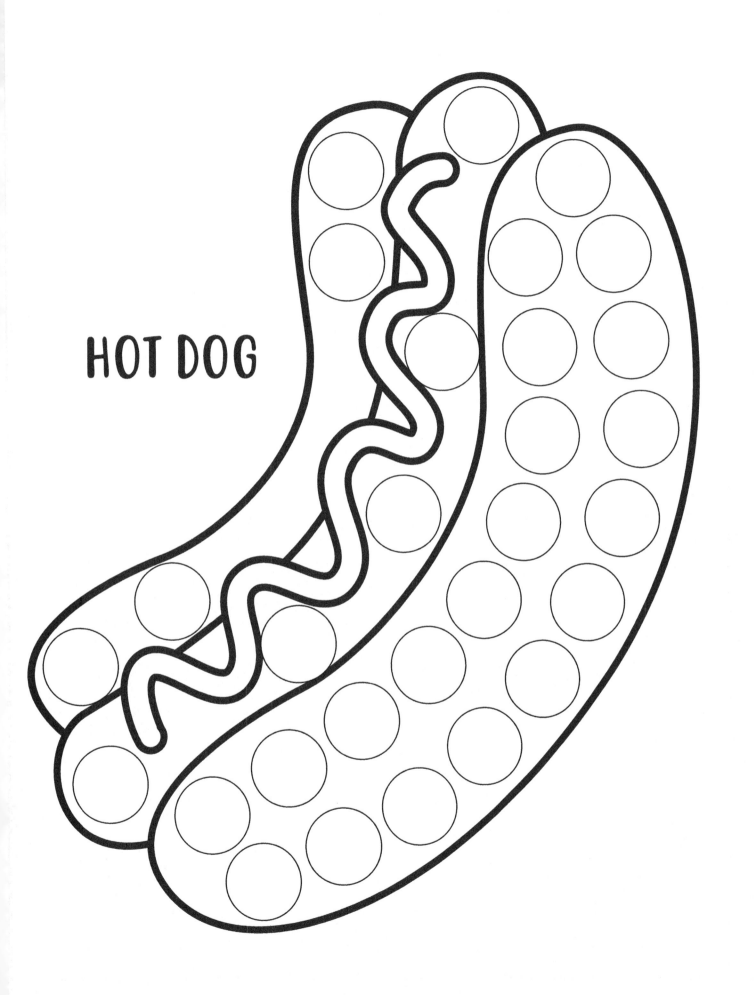

PATRIOTIC HAT

4TH OF JULY

DRUM

FOOTBALL

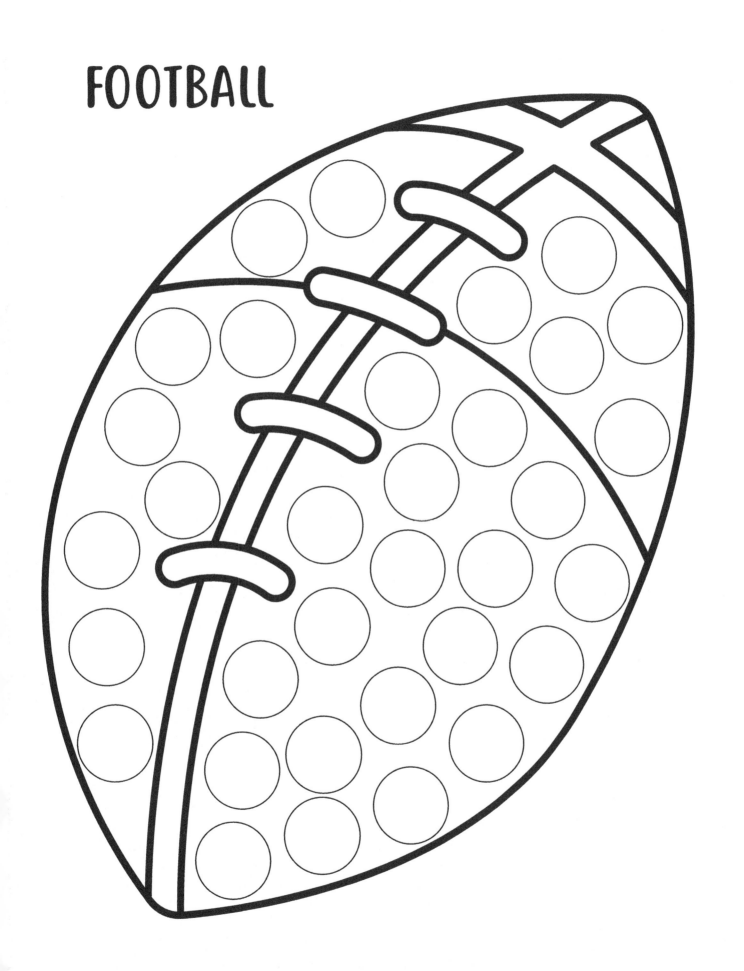

COCKADE

POPCORNS

FLAG

CANDLES

CAKE

PARADE

KITE
IN THE SKY

PINWHEEL

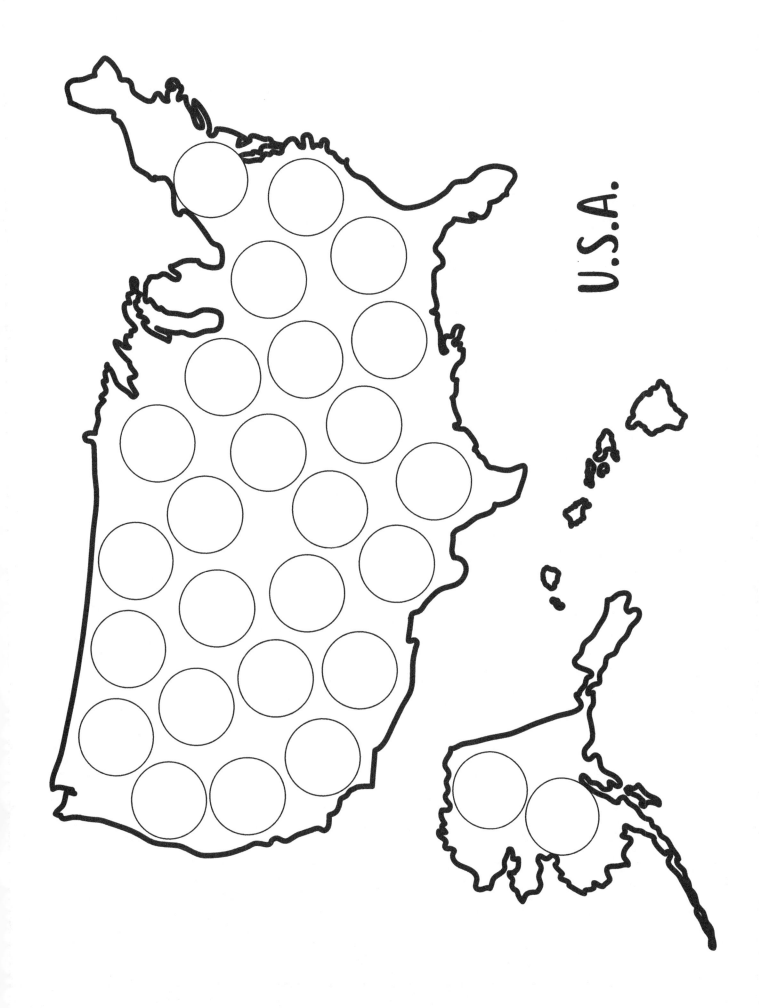

U.S.A.

ICE-CREAM

CUPCAKE

FLIP FLOPS

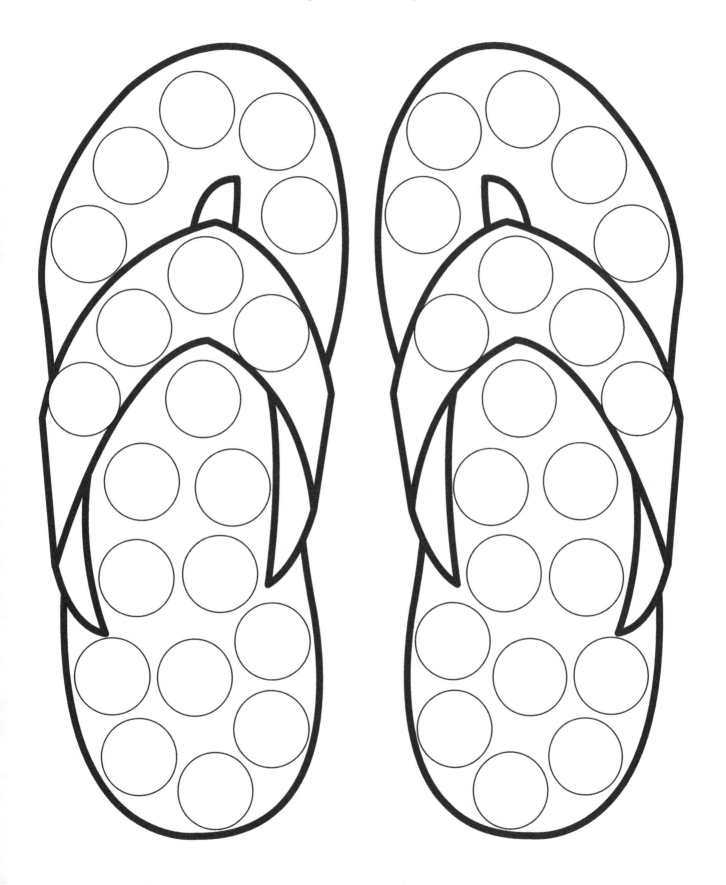

BARBECUE

PICNIC

FIND YOUR WAY TO THE BALLOONS
BY COLORING THE STARS

BALD EAGLE

LOLLIPOP

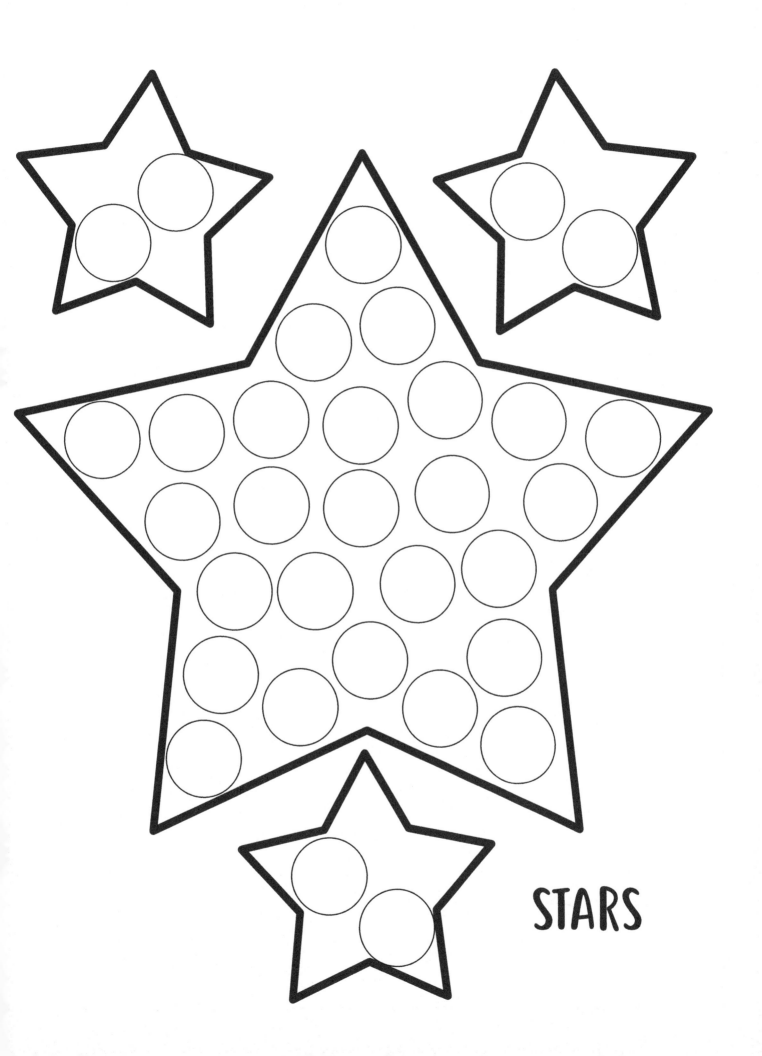

STARS

LIBERTY BELL

STATUE OF LIBERTY

FIREWORKS

COLOR YOUR WAY TO THE FOOD

DID YOU ENJOY THIS BOOK?

Let us know what you think by scanning the QR code below

Share some PICTURES of your ARTWORK with us in your review!

KINDRELL
Land Press

SHARE YOUR ARTWORK WITH US

@KINDRELLLANDPRESS

Made in the USA
Monee, IL
27 June 2022

98729527R00044